Sounds

Words by David Bennett
Pictures by Rosalinda Kightley

A BANTAM LITTLE ROOSTER BOOK

TORONTO · NEW YORK · LONDON · SYDNEY · AUCKLAND

You learn about the world through your five senses.

You can see with your eyes, smell with your nose, taste with your tongue, feel with your skin . . .

. . . and hear all the sounds around you because you have ears.

There are two parts to your ears.
You can see the parts that are outside
your head. But did you know that
part of your ears are inside your head, too?

Ears come in many shapes and sizes.
Rabbits have long, thin ears.
Cats have small, pointed ears.

Birds only have ears inside their head.
Some animals can even turn
their ears toward sounds.

We talk to each other using words.
But different animals make different sounds.

A cow goes moo. A sheep goes baa.

A dog goes woof, woof. And a cat goes meow.
What goes quack, quack? What goes oink, oink?

The sounds you make tell people
and animals how you feel.

You cry when you are sad.

You laugh when you are happy.

Some sounds tell you what to do. When your telephone rings, you know someone wants to talk to you. So you pick it up.

No sound at all might mean that something isn't working.

Loud sounds can be a warning.
A shout or scream can mean someone
needs help.

In an emergency, police cars, fire engines, and ambulances use a loud siren to tell you to keep out of their way.

You can also hear very quiet sounds
like the ticking of a clock or someone whispering.
You can even hear footsteps on a carpet.

If it is very quiet, a sudden sound
can make you jump.

Music is another kind of sound.

Music can change the way you feel.

Loud, happy music makes you want to
sing and dance.
Soft, sad music makes you feel quiet.

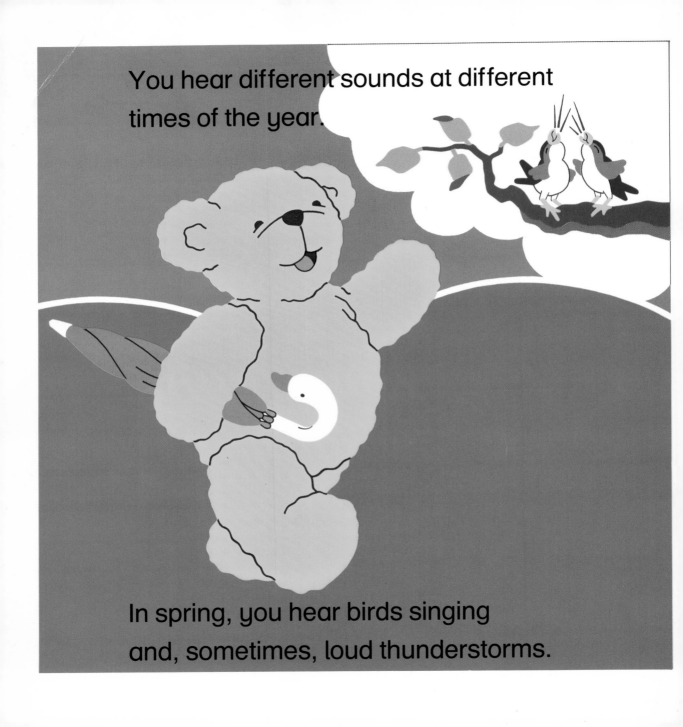

In summer, you hear bees buzzing.

In fall, you hear leaves crunching
under your feet . . . .

But in winter, when the snow falls,
it muffles the sounds, and everything
seems a little quieter.

Can you think of any other
words like this?

buzz

fizz

hiss

sizzle

If you sit very still, you can hear a lot of different sounds all at the same time.

Close your eyes and see how many
sounds you know.

BEAR REVIEW

1. You can hear sounds all around you because you have ears.

2. Part of your ears are outside your head, and part are inside your head.

3. The sounds you make tell people how you feel. Sounds can be loud or soft.

4. Music is a sound. There are different sounds at different times of the year.